BEHIND THE BRAND

YOUTUBE

BY SARA GREEN

BELLWETHER MEDIA • MINNEAPOLIS, MN

Blastoff! Discovery launches a new mission: reading to learn. Filled with facts and features, each book offers you an exciting new world to explore!

BLASTOFF! UNIVERSE

GRADE K

GRADES 1-3

GRADE 4

This edition first published in 2024 by Bellwether Media, Inc.

Library of Congress Cataloging-in-Publication Data

Names: Green, Sara, 1964- author.
Title: YouTube / by Sara Green.
Description: Minneapolis, MN : Bellwether Media, Inc., [2024] | Series:
    Blastoff! Discovery. Behind the brand | Includes bibliographical
    references and index. | Audience: Ages 7-13 | Audience: Grades 4-6 |
    Summary: "Engaging images accompany information about YouTube.
    The combination of high-interest subject matter and narrative text is intended for
    students in grades 3 through 8"– Provided by publisher.
Identifiers: LCCN 2023008905 (print) | LCCN 2023008906 (ebook) |
    ISBN 9798886874495 (library binding) | ISBN 9798886875416
    (paperback) | ISBN 9798886876376 (ebook)
Subjects: LCSH: YouTube (Electronic resource)–Juvenile literature. |
    Internet videos–Juvenile literature. | Online social networks–Juvenile
    literature. | Hurley, Chad, 1977- | Chen, Steve, 1978- | Karim, Jawed,   1979-
Classification: LCC TK5105.8868.Y68 G58 2024 (print) | LCC TK5105.8868.Y68
    (ebook) | DDC 302.30285–dc23/eng/20230302
LC record available at https://lccn.loc.gov/2023008905
LC ebook record available at https://lccn.loc.gov/2023008906

Editor: Betsy Rathburn   Designer: Andrea Schneider

Printed in the United States of America, North Mankato, MN.

TABLE OF
CONTENTS

A SLIMY EXPERIMENT   4

INTRODUCING YOUTUBE!   6

YOUTUBE GROWS   14

SOMETHING FOR EVERYONE   18

YOUTUBE HELPS   26

A YOUTUBE COMMUNITY   28

GLOSSARY   30

TO LEARN MORE   31

INDEX   32

A SLIMY EXPERIMENT

SLIME

A group of friends spends a Saturday afternoon together. They decide to do a science experiment. But what kind? One friend suggests making lip balm. Another wonders if they could turn a potato into a battery. Then, they get another idea. They can make slime! A YouTube video will show them how.

The friends open YouTube on a tablet and start a tutorial. It shows what ingredients they need and what steps to follow. Soon, the friends have a batch of gooey slime. The YouTube video helped make this project easy and fun!

SLIME INGREDIENTS

YOUTUBE TUTORIAL

5

INTRODUCING YOUTUBE!

1000 **YOUTUBE HEADQUARTERS**
SAN BRUNO, CALIFORNIA

▶ YouTube

YouTube is the world's largest video-sharing platform. It is owned by Google. Anyone with a computer or mobile device can watch YouTube videos. YouTube is available in more than 100 countries and can be enjoyed in 80 different languages. In 2022, the company earned almost $30 billion. Its headquarters is in San Bruno, California.

More than 120 million people visit YouTube every day. Many users create channels and upload their own content. Gaming content and product reviews are popular. Tutorials and music videos are other favorites. YouTube also runs YouTube TV, a television streaming service. It offers more than 100 channels, including Disney and PBS Kids.

THE MOST USERS

India has the most YouTube users in the world, with around 467 million users. The United States follows with around 246 million users.

YOUTUBE HEADQUARTERS

SAN BRUNO, CALIFORNIA

The idea for YouTube was sparked in 2004. Steve Chen, Chad Hurley, and Jawed Karim thought videos were too hard to find and share online. They decided to make a video-sharing website to help people find videos more easily.

COWORKERS AND FRIENDS

Steve, Chad, and Jawed worked together at a company called PayPal before they started YouTube.

JAWED KARIM

CHAD HURLEY

STEVE CHEN

FIRST YOUTUBE VIDEO
POSTED BY JAWED

0:12 / 0:19

e zoo

wed ✓
M subscribers

Subscribe

YOUTUBE'S HOME PAGE
IN DECEMBER 2005

You Tube
Upload, tag and share your videos worldwide!
Sign Up | Log In | Help
Home | Videos | Channels | Friends | Upload
My Videos | My Favorites | My Messages | My Subscriptions | My Playlists | My Profile

Search Videos | Search Users

Watch
Instantly find and watch 1000's of fast streaming videos

Upload
Quickly upload and tag videos in

Share
Easily share your videos with

Sign up for your free account!
Nano a Day Giveaway Extended!

Today's Featured Videos...

tokyo
tokyo at night
Tags // tokyo
Channels // Travel & Places

We're giving away a 4GB iPod Nano every day through the end of the year! Increase your chances of winning by:

They launched YouTube on February 14, 2005. That April, Jawed posted the first video. It was 19 seconds long and featured him at the San Diego Zoo. YouTube began to grow quickly. By the official launch in December, there were more than 2 million video views each day!

SEQUOIA CAPITAL
HEADQUARTERS

Viewer numbers continued to climb. A company called Sequoia Capital helped YouTube grow even more. It put a total of $11.5 million into the company. By March 2006, more than 25 million videos were available on YouTube. More were being uploaded every day.

AN EARLY HIT!

A 2005 Nike advertisement featuring the Brazilian soccer player Ronaldinho was the first YouTube video to get 1 million views!

YouTube's growth was exciting, but it also created problems. The company needed more computer equipment and faster internet to keep up with video uploads. YouTube also faced legal problems. It did not have the rights to host some videos online. The owners of the videos were upset. Because of these problems, the three founders decided to sell YouTube.

EARLY YOUTUBE HITS

	YEAR CREATED	NUMBER OF VIEWS AS OF MARCH 2023
EVOLUTION OF DANCE	**2006**	**311 MILLION**
OTTERS HOLDING HANDS	**2007**	**22 MILLION**
KEYBOARD CAT!	**2007**	**71 MILLION**
SKATEBOARDING DOG	**2007**	**22 MILLION**
DAVID AFTER DENTIST	**2009**	**141 MILLION**

Susan Wojcicki, a leader at Google, thought YouTube would be a great addition to Google. Google's attempt to make a popular video-sharing website had failed. Susan believed that YouTube would succeed. She convinced Google's other leaders to buy YouTube. In November 2006, Google bought YouTube for $1.65 billion.

SUSAN WOJCICKI

BORN July 5, 1968, in California

ROLE Leader of YouTube from 2014 to 2023

ACCOMPLISHMENTS

Convinced Google to buy YouTube and later, as its leader, helped YouTube grow

GOOGLE HEADQUARTERS

Google and YouTube began to work together as a team. YouTube received more resources to update its equipment. It also got help from Google to solve its legal problems. Google made deals with entertainment companies. YouTube removed videos the companies did not want posted. With the help of Google, YouTube continued growing!

YOUTUBE GROWS

Getaway Event
hyundaiusa.com
Shop now

Ad 2 of 2 · 0:09 ⓘ hyundaiusa.com

ADVERTISEMENT ON YOUTUBE

0:05 / 0:15

In 2007, YouTube launched new versions in nine countries. That year, YouTube also began its Partner Program. It let popular YouTubers make money from their videos. The creators placed advertisements in their videos and earned money based on the number of views. By 2012, anyone with 1,000 subscribers could join. The program inspired more people to become YouTubers. Some, such as Justin Bieber, became superstars!

Advertising continued to grow as YouTube's main source of income. By the end of 2008, most of YouTube's $200 million yearly earnings came from ads!

CAN YOU BELIEBE IT?

Justin Bieber is one of the first musicians to gain fame on YouTube. He first started posting videos in 2007. His most popular videos now have billions of views!

TAY ZONDAY, AN EARLY PARTNER PROGRAM MEMBER

YouTube leaders looked for other ways to earn money. They kicked off a paid subscription service in 2014 with Music Key. This service let users stream music videos with no ads. The next year, the service became YouTube Red. It let subscribers access all videos ad-free! In 2018, YouTube replaced YouTube Red with YouTube Premium. YouTube Premium includes many benefits, such as ad-free videos and music, offline viewing, and more.

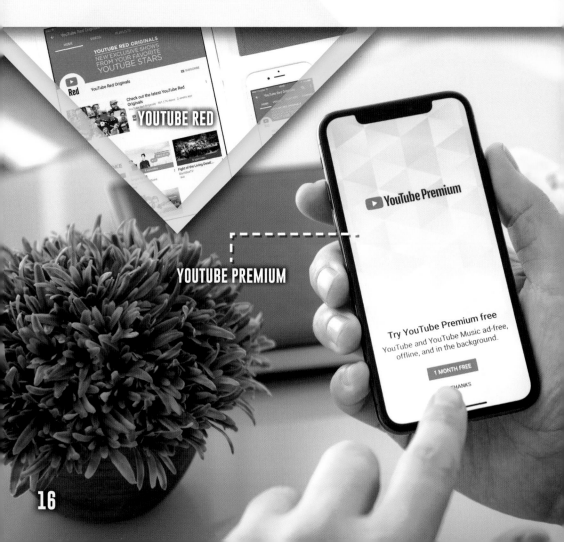

YOUTUBE RED

YOUTUBE PREMIUM

YOUTUBE KIDS
MOBILE APP

YouTube took another important step in 2015. It launched the YouTube Kids mobile **app**. Kids could safely watch family-friendly videos, listen to music, and learn new skills on YouTube!

MEGA HIT!

In December 2012, the music video for the song "Gangnam Style" by PSY became the first YouTube video to get more than 1 billion views!

SOMETHING FOR EVERYONE

Today, YouTube is among the most popular websites. There are around 800 million videos on YouTube. The biggest YouTube channels have more than 150 million subscribers. Every day, viewers around the world watch about 1 billion hours of video in total!

YouTube continues to offer new features. It rolled out YouTube Shorts in 2020. This service lets people easily use their mobile devices to watch and create videos up to a minute long. YouTube Shorts are very popular. They get more than 50 billion views every day!

UPLOAD FRENZY!

More than 700,000 hours of video are uploaded to YouTube every day!

MINECRAFT

YouTube videos cover a wide range of topics. Tutorials show viewers how to do almost anything. The Art for Kids Hub channel shows kids how to draw, paint, and more. Karina Garcia's videos teach kids how to make slime. DanTDM is a popular gaming channel created by Daniel Middleton. He reacts to video games such as *Minecraft* and gives tips about gameplay.

Many kids tune in to learning channels. BrainPop and TED-Ed cover subjects such as history, science, and more. SciShow Kids is all about science and the natural world. Its videos about spiders, worms, and blobfish have millions of views!

KARINA GARCIA

DANIEL MIDDLETON

21

Some of YouTube's most popular videos are made by kids! Ryan Kaji is the star of the Ryan's World channel. Ryan reviews toys, shows pranks, and does science experiments. He is one of the most popular kids on YouTube!

POPULAR EDUCATIONAL CHANNELS

NUMBER OF SUBSCRIBERS (AS OF MARCH 2023)

Channel	Subscribers
BRIGHT SIDE	MORE THAN 44 MILLION
RYAN'S WORLD	MORE THAN 34 MILLION
TED-ED	MORE THAN 18 MILLION
NETFLIX JR.	MORE THAN 13 MILLION
ART FOR KIDS HUB	MORE THAN 6 MILLION

CHANNEL NAME

Subscribe

ANASTASIA
RADZINSKAYA

RYAN KAJI

Anastasia Radzinskaya, known as Nastya, has a YouTube channel called Like Nastya. Her videos are filled with fun, upbeat content. Evan Breeze is another popular creator. Millions of people subscribe to his channel, EvanTubeHD. Evan became popular for reviewing LEGO sets and other toys. He also participates in challenges and science experiments. Kid YouTubers bring smiles to viewers around the world!

Users can visit new places in **virtual reality** videos. They can wear a special headset and see 360-degree views of museums, mountains, and even space! Future content made with **artificial intelligence** (AI) may become more common. Creators tell AI what to make. Viewers get to see the results!

YouTube content is entertaining, but it is not always safe for kids. YouTube uses AI to remove harmful content. In 2020, AI removed 11 million videos. Features such as Supervised Experiences also help kids stay safe. It lets parents choose which content their kids see. YouTube works hard to keep people both entertained and safe!

VIRTUAL REALITY
HEADSET

YOUTUBE TIMELINE

2005
YouTube is launched

2006
Google buys YouTube for $1.65 billion

2007
Ads are first used on YouTube

2017
YouTube TV is launched

2021
A safety feature called Supervised Experiences is released

2005
The first video is posted to YouTube

2012
The music video for "Gangnam Style" becomes the first video to reach 1 billion views

2007
The Partner Program is launched

2018
YouTube Premium replaces YouTube Red

2023
Susan Wojcicki steps down as YouTube's leader

A GOOD MATCH!

AI matches viewers with videos they will probably enjoy. It creates video suggestions based on a viewer's video-watching history!

YOUTUBE HELPS

YOUTUBE CHARITY EVENT

YouTube not only hosts videos. It also helps people give back! YouTube Giving allows YouTubers to support charities they care about. They host fundraisers on their videos or live streams. Viewers can click a button to give money to different causes. For example, a 2019 fundraiser raised $500,000 in 24 hours for My Friend's Place. This organization helps homeless youth.

A WORTHY CHANNEL

YouTube Social Impact is a channel that features videos about the environment, education, and other causes.

YouTube's owner, Google, also raises money for many causes. Since 2015, the company has given over $45 million to help refugees. Google also gave $100 million in response to the COVID-19 pandemic. The money helps fight the disease and care for people affected by it.

GIVING BACK

$500,000
RAISED IN FUNDRAISER FOR MY FRIEND'S PLACE IN 2019

MORE THAN
$45 MILLION
GIVEN TO HELP REFUGEES

$100 MILLION
GIVEN TO FIGHT COVID-19

A YOUTUBE COMMUNITY

VIDCON

Many YouTube fans and creators attend special conventions. VidCon is one of the most popular. This event helps creators learn to improve their channels. It lets fans meet their favorite YouTubers, ask questions, and take photos. All guests can play games, take part in special events, and browse fun displays!

VIDCON

WHAT IT IS

Convention where YouTube creators and fans meet each other and learn how to create and improve content

FIRST HAPPENED

2010

WHEN IT HAPPENS

Yearly

WHERE IT IS

Anaheim, California

NUMBER OF ATTENDEES

Around 50,000

YouTube camps also help fans take part in YouTube. Kids attend camps to learn how to use cameras, edit their videos, and grow their channels. YouTube has changed the way millions of people share and view videos. Almost everyone can find something to enjoy on YouTube!

GLOSSARY

advertisements—public notices that tell people about products, services, or events

app—a program such as a game or internet browser; an app is also called an application.

artificial intelligence—a computer's ability to do things a human mind can do

charities—organizations that help others in need

conventions—events where fans of a subject meet

founders—the people who created a company

fundraisers—events where money is raised for specific causes

headquarters—a company's main office

pandemic—an outbreak of a disease over a whole country or the world

platform—an app or other software on which people can watch and share videos

refugees—people who flee their countries to escape war or violence

rights—a legal claim to something

subscribers—people who sign up for something in order to get easy access to its content

tutorial—a book, video, or other media that teaches people how to do something

virtual reality—related to a type of computer program that makes users feel like they are somewhere that does not exist